FAMILY ALBUM:
AN ILLUSTRATED GLIMPSE

Family Album:
An Illustrated Glimpse

Prose and Poems by
PEDRO XAVIER SOLÍS

Translated by
DIANE NEUHAUSER

Illustrated by
MELISSA WARP

Adelaide Books
New York/Lisbon
2019

FAMILY ALBUM: AN ILLUSTRATED GLIMPSE
Prose and Poems
By Pedro Xavier Solís

Translated by Diane Neuhauser

Illustrated by Melissa Warp

Copyright © by Pedro Xavier Solís
Cover design © 2019 Adelaide Books

Published by Adelaide Books, New York / Lisbon
adelaidebooks.org

Editor-in-Chief
Stevan V. Nikolic

All rights reserved. No part of this book may be reproduced in any manner whatsoever without written permission from the author except in the case of brief quotations embodied in critical articles and reviews.

For any information, please address Adelaide Books
at info@adelaidebooks.org

or write to:

Adelaide Books
244 Fifth Ave. Suite D27
New York, NY, 10001

ISBN: 978-1-951896-78-2

Printed in the United States of America

Contents

Translator's Introduction **7**

The Man **9**
    Clairvoyant **11**
    The Egg **15**
    The Harshness Noted **17**
    Sonnet Searching for Light **19**
    Street Within **21**
    Photos of the Wedding Cake **25**
    Bipolarity **29**

The Father **31**
    My Little Solitary One **33**
    On Board **37**
    Blue **39**
    Little Bird **43**
    Earthworm Friends **47**
    The Sculpture **49**
    The Angel **51**

Bored **55**
Questions After the Divorce **58**
The Box of Crayons from the Heart of my Son **61**
On How Bright Light Occurred in the Darkness **65**

On Death and Consolation **67**
The Jar of Caramels **69**
Portrait in the Garden **73**
Choice **76**
What Was Said by the Samurai's Woman **79**
Revolution of the Butterflies **83**
The Consolation of Poetry **85**

About the Authors **87**

Translator's Introduction

Living in Nicaragua is a world apart from our typical experience in North America: The sounds alone let you know instantly this place is unique. You wake to birds that do not just twitter, but screech and trill entire multi-stanza songs. There are processions with tubas blasting, dogs always barking somewhere, firecrackers going off for any excuse of a holiday. And of course, everywhere the vegetative excess of the tropics, where vines with huge blue flowers don't just cover a trellis, but instead the entire side of a house.

Pedro Xavier grew up in Nicaragua, surrounded by family and books. His grandfather, Pablo Antonio Cuadra, was a poet and intellectual leader of his time, with books and art in every corner. His mother's house now includes Pedro Xavier's personal library, where he has a desk and pathways through a collection covering several generations of family obsessions with reading. The houses they share are surrounded by gardens, patios with wicker rocking chairs, and, mercifully, fans—it is hot. By midday, the heat shimmers a golden green.

And then there is a presence of water: fountains, two sea coasts, and one of the largest freshwater lakes in the hemisphere, existing in constant contrast to the fierce blaze of the sun. And amidst all this sensual onslaught are people who embrace even the gringa stranger, who seem to live at significant levels of passionate engagement, whether personal or political.

In one sense, these poems are snapshots of a particular life in Nicaragua, perspectives on a person who thinks deeply—about everything! Pedro Xavier has been passionate about putting democracy into action in his county, dedicating many years to that end, with significant disappointments along the way. He is also dedicated to the literary vitality of Nicaragua through his research, his career as an editor, his participation on boards, and of course, his writing This collection of his poems offers a way of reflecting on the family album each of us creates through the daily actions of our lives.

The Man

In this selection of poems and prose, I have tried to show key aspects of the man who is introverted; cerebral with a sly sense of humor; a voracious reader as a means for appeasing his curiosity. Most importantly he is a person who cares deeply about his family, his country, and the burdensome responsibility of being human. DN

El vidente

De pronto, sin augurarlo ni previo aviso, empezó a ver a las personas en su esqueleto. Diferían menos unos de otros, pues la carne nos distingue con rasgos personales. Parecían más rudos, pues la carne marca al cuerpo con su suavidad. Y más bien le resultaba todo el asunto bastante repelente. No se acepta fácilmente que el otro se destape las facciones de la muerte. Es inherente a tu natural que te sea repulsivo. Daban lo mismo la muchacha joven y la mujer entrada en años, una vez despojadas del orgullo de la carne; el taxista, el niño lustrador, la marchanta o el mendigo que, en los esponsales de la necesidad, extendía los huesos de su mano. Creyó que estaba volviéndose loco. Optó por hablar con la cabeza gacha, bajando la vista para evitar mirar de frente a las calaveras que le dirigían la palabra. De pronto, tal como vino, la visión se fue. Pero ya se le había revelado que, a flor de piel, había una realidad obsequiosamente subyacente. No por menos visible, menos verdadera. No por descarnada, más terrible.

(Variación del cuadro "Hans Burgkmair y su esposa Anna" de Lukas Furtenagel).

Clairvoyant

Suddenly, without warning or foresight, I began to see everyone as skeletons. They differed less, one from another, since the flesh creates the unique image of a person. They seemed more coarse, since the flesh covers the body with softness. And more than that, the whole thing was rather repellent. It's not so easy to accept that others could uncover the features of their death. It's normal that it would be repulsive. The young girl and the woman advanced in age appeared the same, once they were stripped of their pride of flesh: the taxi driver, the shoe shine boy, the merchant or the beggar, as they went about their work, extended the bones of their hand. I thought I was going crazy. I decided to speak with my head down, lowering my view so that I didn't have to look at the skulls where I directed my words. Suddenly, just like it came, the visions went away. But now it had been revealed that, under the bloom of the skin, obsequiously lies another reality. For being less visible, it's not less true. For being more fleshy, more terrible.

(Variation on the painting "Hans Burgkmair and His Wife" by Lukas Furtenagel)

El huevo

El huevo no siempre me pareció incómodo.
Todo extremadamente limpio y bien dispuesto.
Cierta tibieza contribuía al equilibrio interior,
aunque el horizonte era un insistente cascarón blanco.
Pero el huevo acaba estorbando cuando se piensa en volar.
Entonces rompí el cascarón.
         Fuera de él
extraño la seguridad de sus paredes blancas,
el dogmático orden, la rutina que me exasperaba.
No es que el horizonte sea ahora un cascarón roto.
Simplemente pienso en el huevo
cada vez que trato en vano de remontar vuelo
retozando entre las matas con otras lagartijas.

The Egg

The egg didn't always seem uncomfortable to me.
All extremely clean and well proportioned.
A tepid coolness contributed to the equilibrium inside,
even though the horizon was this persistent white shell.
But it ended up as a barrier when I considered flying.

So I broke the shell.
          Outside of it
I missed the security of its white walls,
the dogmatic order, the exasperating routine.
It's not that the horizon now is a broken shell:
simply that I think about the egg
each time I try in vain to fly
twisting around in the grass with the other geckos.

El aspereza notada

> *Mas solamente aquella*
> *fuerza de tu beldad sería cantada*
> *y alguna vez con ella*
> *también sería notada*
> *el aspereza de que estás armada.*
>
> Garcilaso de la Vega

> *Juro que esta mujer me ha partido los sesos*
> Gonzalo Rojas

Mejor sería que no la hubiera requerido amores.
Me despojó la armadura sin mediar armisticio.
Le entregué greba, almete, coraza. Errores.
Ahora tienen sus armas donde aplicar su filo.

The Harshness Noted

                  But only with that strike
          of your singular beauty so exalted
                    and at times quite alike
                      would surely be noted
the harshness of which you are appointed.

                    Garcilaso de la Vega

I swear this woman has driven me senseless!
                    Gonzalo Rojas

How much better it would be if I hadn't needed affection.
I relinquished my armor without negotiating an armistice.
Handed over leg plates, helmet, body shield. Miscalculation.
Now her weapons are where she can apply the worst kind of
justice.

Soneto buscando la luz

¿Por qué si tanto amor profeso
y en él madruga tanta dicha,
tiene en vez mi alma mal suceso
y la voluntad en agonía?

¿Por qué, peregrino del camino,
pierdo la ruta a cada paso
al poco andar ya me fatigo
y dejo a medias lo que acabo?

¿Cómo sustentar la vida mía
si mi equipaje es vanidad
y en vez de vida, muerte aliño?

Hoy quiero vaciar mi levedad:
yo, del engaño peón ladino,
quiero luz cabal de mediodía.

Sonnet Searching for Light

Why, if I go on so professing love
and with it, such good fortune finds me,
do I instead have my soul undone
and my will, agonized unceasingly?

Why, seeker on the road to devotion,
do I lose the way with each step
with little effort tire to exhaustion
and leave half done what I attempt?

How to continue with this life of mine
if my baggage is vanity
and I pack it with death instead of life?

Today, I want to be rid of my banality:
I, a man of deceit and artifice,
want the most exacting light to shine.

Calle adentro

Yo me había venido llenando de calles interiores
      que no me llevaban a ningún sitio.
Por aquí se abría una trocha que desembocaba en
      una fábrica fantasma de cristales molidos.
Otra conducía a un punto ciego con un letrero
      que decía: "Se acopian causas perdidas".
Más acá, una avenida topaba con un desvencijado
      taller de refacción llamado La Esperanza.

Pero donde había añicos, ella fue formando un mosaico.
Y donde había derrota, redimió el sentido
      de mis causas perdidas.
Y en La Esperanza me quitó la hoja de higo y
      me dio leche y miel bajo su lengua.

Hasta que un día me dijo que se iba en un viaje sin regreso.
Su escala de Managua estaba concluida.

Entonces cada cosa tornó a su punto de partida.
Y volví a la realidad de unos días sin relieve
y de unas calles que hago para que nadie las transite.

La Esperanza volvió a ser tan mortecina como antes.
Mis causas perdidas son una paleta de colores desvaídos.
Y la penumbra malhiere los viejos fragmentos de un mosaico.

(Marzo 2009)

Street Within

I had become full of interior streets
that failed to lead me anywhere.
From here a track started that arrived at
a ghost factory of shattered crystals.
Another proceeded to a blind point with a sign
that said, "Gather here for dead ends."
Over there, an avenue ran into a ramshackle
repair shop named The Hope.

But where there were shards, she made a mosaic.
And where defeat, she redeemed meaning in my lost causes.
In The Hope, she removed the fig leaf,
gave me milk and honey from under her tongue.

Until the day she told me of her trip with no return.
Her stopover in Managua had come to an end.

Then every thing turned back to its starting point.
I returned to the days of unrelieved inwardness
and to the streets I make so that no one enters.

The Hope became moribund like before.
My lost causes are a palette of faded colors.
And dark shadows dissipate the fragments of mosaic.

March, 2009

Fotos del pastel de la boda

Una mano fina de mujer levanta la figura
caída del hombrecito vestido de frac
y estampado aviesamente de bruces
en el tercer piso glaseado del queque,
puesto sobre el mantel de lino blanco
de la mesa central. La mano samaritana
quiere enderezarlo, restaurar el ornato,
la lógica decorativa, y atajar las conjeturas
inevitables del suceso: la irrisión, la mala
levadura de la gente. En una foto siguiente,
junto a la huella en el baño del pastel
(la premonición), debidamente erguida
y alcorzada reaparece la pareja de
efigiecitas con sus testas de alcornoque.

Photos of the Wedding Cake

A woman's slender hand lifts the fallen
figure of the tiny man dressed in a tux,
perversely imprinted face down
in the icing on the third tier of the cake,
which rests on a white linen tablecloth
of the center table. The helpful hand
wants to set it right, to restore order
(the decorative logic) and intercept the gossip
inevitable with these events: the derision,
a gloom spreading over all. In the next photo,
by the imprint in the cake's frosting
(a premonition) the effigies reappear,
shakily upright and stuck in place,
the couple with their cork heads.

Bipolaridad

Hay días en que su mente amanece como una jaula abierta
de la que brotan gorjeos de pájaros alzando sus alas
revoloteando y piando sobre las copas altas de los árboles,
libre jolgorio sin derrotero, sólo luz y canto y vuelo.

Otros días su mente zozobra en lo profundo del corazón
como un barco anegado en la obscuridad del lecho marino
con un coro de fantasmas cantando en la noche sorda
echado a pique, proa encallada, sin velas ni quilla ni ruta.

Bipolarity

Some days your mind opens like a sprung cage
with birds breaking away, chirping, flapping their wings
fluttering and swooping over the high green of trees
free revelry without limit, only light and song and flight.

Other days your mind capsizes into the depth of your heart
like a boat inundated in the darkness of the sea bed
with a chorus of ghosts singing in the deaf night
sunken, prow encased, without sail or keel or direction

The Father

Pedro Xavier has five children and worked extensively with his grandfather, the poet Pablo Antonio Cuadra. When we visited his grandparents house in Managua, Pedro Xavier walked from room to room, "This is where my mother stayed while she was building her house down the street, and here is where my oldest son lived for several years, and…" Houses are places for extended family, and home will always be made ready. DN

Mi pequeño solitario

… a mi hijo Mauricio

> *"Y llamó a su hijo Gerson,*
> *que significa extranjero,*
> *porque Moisés dijo:*
> *soy un extranjero en esta tierra".*
>
> Éxodo 2, 22

My Little Solitary One

…to my son Mauricio*

> *And he called his son Gerson,*
> *which meant stranger,*
> *because Moses said:*
> *"I am a stranger in this land."*
>
> Exodus 2:22

*Translator's note: The prose poems on pages 36-55 are from a larger collection, which offers tribute to the creative brilliance of those on the autism spectrum.

Abordo

Un aire sin alas sopla en el mar verdísimo del patio. El sol salpica el musgo del árbol en el que Gerson, como en una lancha atada a sus raíces, sumerge sus brumosas soledades. Busca en la lejanía la luz de la atalaya, sin romper el silencio de aquella mar sin estelas. El aire sopla por la popa hundida del árbol, moviendo levemente los obenques del bejuco. En lontananza, bajo el sol sangrante, mueve su cola un perro de ojos azules que se acerca hasta la punta más baja de estribor. La faz del timonel resplandece. –"Celeste", la llama dulcemente, volviendo a poner pie en el puerto que había abandonado.

On Board

A breeze without wings blows across the deep green sea of the patio. The sun splashes on the moss of the tree where Gerson, in his boat anchored by roots, submerges into the shade of his solitary refuge. He searches in the distance for a lighthouse beacon, without disturbing the silence of that wakeless sea. A breeze crosses the stern, sunken into the tree, slowly moving the rigging of vines and reeds. At a distance, under the bleeding sun, moves the tail of a dog with blue eyes, as it approaches the lower starboard point. The face of the helmsman lights up: "Blue," he calls fondly, returning to put foot on the shore he had abandoned.

Celeste

Gerson se recuesta sobre el pasto de color inmóvil y jade, tranquilo como un infante en el sueño. Los follajes gorjean de pájaros. Las ramas se mueven como una bandada de ángeles rústicos. Poco a poco se repliega el paisaje diurno, y en los ojos de Gerson abrevan nuevas invenciones y espejos silentes. Los menudos luminares del cielo son lanzas contorsionadas, huestes de Dios cuya espada no puede ser abatida... la luna en creciente de plata es un reloj de bolsillo que pende de la bóveda oscura... En el refugio de sus pensares solitarios, Gerson divisa una atalaya. Y montándose en un árbol, en la caleta de hojarasca –sin corriente, ni orilla opuesta, ni agua– guía su pensado esquife. Celeste, que no advierte la dimensión de la aventura, le mordisquea el tobillo echando a pique su travesía introvertida. "¡Celeste!", grita, y salta sobre ella retornando de su Mar Océano anchísimo; pero Celeste, con mayor audacia y edad, lo empuja en el pecho con las patas tumbándolo sobre la grama y le lame la cara en un gozo sin fin. Celeste perturba incesantemente las fantasías de Gerson. Las transfigura en ladridos y constelaciones terrestres.

Blue

On the grass, a color quiescent and jade, Gerson lies as tranquil as a sleeping infant. The foliage warbles with birds. The branches move like a multitude of sylvan angels. Little by little the everyday panorama retracts, and Gerson's eyes drink in new inventions and silent mirrors. The bits and pieces of bright light from the sky become a tangle of spears, an army from God whose weapons cannot be defeated… the silver crescent of the moon is a pocket watch that hangs from the dark heavens. In the refuge of his solitary thoughts, Gerson detects a lighthouse. And mounting a tree, ensconced in the cover of leaves, without waves or water or opposite shore, he guides his imagined skiff. Blue, who fails to grasp the magnitude of the adventure, is nibbling at Gerson's ankles causing his introverted voyage to founder. "Blue!" he shouts, and jumps at her, returning from his wide Ocean Sea. But Blue, with more audacity and age, pushes him on the chest with her paws, tumbling him over the grass, and licks his face with endless joy. Blue incessantly disrupts Gerson's reveries. She transforms them into barking and terrestrial confabulations.

El pajarito

Su rifle de palo se había estropeado. Y Gerson había puesto berrinche. Le distrajo de su corajina un pajarito que entró hasta la sala donde se encontraba, y que asustado apuró vuelo hecho un nervio, dándose contra la puerta corrediza de vidrio intentando infructuosamente la huida, chocando en su reconcomio sin encontrar la salida, aunque la ventana permanecía abierta con el lozano paraje de fondo. Al fin, extenuado, divisó ese trozo azul que tenía mayor intensidad que todo el cielo, y alzó alas al aire en pampa. Y a Gerson, volviendo en sí de su malcriadez, le pareció escuchar la voz del ángel que le decía: "Siéntete libre".

Little Bird

His stick rifle had shattered, and Gerson was throwing a temper tantrum. A little bird distracted him from his outrage by entering the room, and in its fright, flew frantically around, hitting against the sliding glass door, desperately attempting escape without success, even though a window was open to lush foliage in the garden. Finally, exhausted, the bird spotted a sliver of blue that had the intensity of all the sky, and winged its way to the air outside. Gerson, returning to himself from his misbehavior, seemed to hear the voice of an angel that said, "Find yourself free."

Los amigos gusanos

Gerson –aún desde la atalaya de su breve edad– solía pensar en la muerte, pues en su navío no temía tocar la otra ribera. La muerte nos pone rostro a tierra, a nivel del *humus*, es decir, nos hace humildes. Reconocer la realidad cotidiana de la muerte humilla la vanidad, esa que nos hace infatuarnos por nuestros pequeños éxitos o nos hace abatirnos por las cosas pasajeras. Y así Gerson monologaba –sin turbarse– con los gusanos, los inminentes huéspedes.

Earthworm Friends

Gerson—even from the purview of his brief years—used to think about death, so that on his boat he had no fear of arriving at the other shore. Death puts us with our face to the ground at the level of *humus*, that is, it makes us humble. To recognize the daily reality of death diminishes the vanity that infatuates us with our small successes or depresses us with passing things. And so Gerson talked—with no distress—to the earthworms, his imminent hosts.

La escultura

Una sonriente figurilla precolombina capta la atención de Gerson: los espejismos de arcilla adentro de sus ojos vigilantes transfiguran su cara como una máscara que lo aproxima y lo aleja, y lo hace siempre aledaño y abismal, como un pozo sin fondo del que siempre sale agua. Por un instante el niño y la artesanía totonaca se hacen cómplices a través del tiempo y el espacio. Se diría que este ser de terracota, hallado en un entierro veracruzano secundario, está hecho para este instante en las postrimerías del siglo XX. ¿La risa es una ofrenda funeraria? Ambos se hacen contemporáneos, sosteniendo la eternidad en una mueca y confabulando ante el mismo despeñadero… y la cabecita sonriente agita su magia y cascabeleo secreto como desde un espejo.

The Sculpture

A smiling pre-Columbian figure captures the attention of Gerson: the allure in its vigilant clay eyes transfigures the face into a mask that approaches and then becomes remote; makes it always close and yet uncontained, like a bottomless well with constantly flowing water. For an instant, the boy and the Totonac artifact make themselves accomplices across time and space. We could say that this terracotta figure, discovered in a secondary burial ground in Veracruz, was made for this instant in the final years of the twentieth century. Perhaps the smile is a funeral offering? They are now contemporaneous, sustaining eternity in a grin and conspiring in front of the same precipice… and the little smiling head stirs up its magic and secret tinkling as if from a reflection.

El ángel

De pronto en el aire de la noche sintió aquel olor de lo invisible, de lo inaccesible, pero que ya le era familiar. Desde detrás de las estrellas, con su apariencia de "agua erguida a contraluz", descendió en los solitarios juegos de Gerson. "Mimados de la Creación", los llamó Rilke. La mirada del ángel era de misericordia hacia los gestos humanos, sus ojos estremecidos de ver la guerra de la ceniza; pero sonreía haciendo lentos signos con su alma al ver a Gerson desgajar una naranja, y movía sus alas con la naturalidad de un ave, pero con más donaire, quitándose el rocío de las plumas bajo el capote del cielo. (Pues éste era el ángel que salvó a los tres jóvenes en el horno –Ananías, Azarías y Misael– con la lluvia de rocío, y Nabucodonosor, que imperaba en el reino, fue confundido). El polen amistoso del ángel caía sobre Gerson, formando una aureola dulce y apacible. Librado de su siglo pero no de sus travesuras, el niño destejía la alpargata de algodón de nube del ángel. Era la atmósfera de los ángeles. Rechazado en el convivio de los hombres, se aposentaba en la alegría soleada de Gerson. Y cantaba suavemente: "¡Santo, Santo, Santo, el Señor Dios Sabaoth!"… y así el niño aprendía a conocer la Ciudad en la noche iluminada, mientras los gallos subidos en los árboles pregonaban otra luz cercana.

The Angel

Suddenly in the night air he sensed that aroma of the invisible, of the inaccessible, which had become familiar to him. From beyond the stars, with its appearance of "uplifted luminous water," the angel descended into Gerson's solitary games.

(Angels were named the pampered darlings of creation by Rilke.)

The gaze of the angel was one of mercy for our human foibles; its eyes trembled at the destruction of war, but smiled with lingering affection from its soul as Gerson pulled apart the sections of an orange. It moved with the natural grace of a bird, but had greater elegance, leaving dew from its wings under the heavenly cloak.

(This same angel saved the three youths –Hanania, Mishael, and Azaria—from the blazing furnace with a rain of dew, causing King Nebuchadnezzar great bewilderment.)

The friendly pollen of the angel fell over Gerson, forming a sweetly serene halo. Freed from this place in time but not from his mischievousness, the child unwove the braided sandal from the cloud of the household angel: this was the atmosphere of the angels. Denied the camaraderie of men, the angel hovered in the solitary joy of Gerson. The angel sang softly, Holy, holy, holy is the Lord of hosts!... and so the child learned to understand the City of God in the luminous night, while the roosters in the trees announced another less distant light.

Aburrido

Por un instante Gerson se aburre. ¿Se apesadumbra?
No columbra el mar verde en el patio, ni las hojas caen
como penachos de espuma, ni hay sombras aladas en las
cumbres de los árboles. La costumbre es la sombra del ser.
Pero unas hebras de nube se dispersan, rutilando entre
el ramaje la luz rosada del sol. Y Celeste sobresaltada –al
modo de un pensar– convoca al mundo imprevisto.

Bored

For an instant, Gerson found himself bored. Was he weighed down with sadness? He couldn't envision the green sea on the patio or the falling leaves like plumes of sea spray; the fluttering shadows in the treetops had disappeared. Habit becomes the darkness of being. But a strand of clouds dispersed, with pink sun shining brightly through the branches. And Blue startled—like the jolt of a thought— summoning an unexpected world.

Preguntas después del divorcio

Eran unos ojos tan hondamente tristes,
que no me van a abandonar jamás.
Su fragilidad profunda le ceñí bien apretada a la mía.
Tenía su voz esa impronta del dolor
en busca de una palabra que le diera seguridad
en medio del mar océano de mi incertidumbre.

–Papi, ¿cómo es que nada nos va a separar
si todo lo llena tu ausencia y dejaste
sin aliñar mi maleta en el ropero?

–Papi, ¿cuál nueva ilusión me va a llevar
al lado de tu cama, si ya no estás en las mañanas
para abrazarte como antes?

–Papi, ¿cuándo vamos a volver a desayunar
como toda mi vida, con vos a distancia de mi mano
pasándome el pan o la mantequilla?

–¿Cómo hago para tenerte al alcance de mi voz
papi, acércame el cereal,
papi, ayúdame con los cordones de los zapatos?

–Papi, tu bendición antes de irme al colegio
¿cómo hago para seguirla recibiendo
en mi frente recién bañada?

–Papi, y al regresar de clases,
¿cómo recupero la alegría de escuchar
el taconeo de tus pasos tras los ladridos de la Lisa
cuando llegabas a abrirme la puerta?

–Papi, cuando en la noche cierro mis ojos sin haberte visto,
me pregunto: ¿qué pasa que todo se me hizo mitades,
como mi corazón partido…?

Questions After the Divorce

There were these eyes so deeply sad,
that they will never leave me.
His profound fragility I bound so tightly to my own.
His voice, this infusion of pain
in search of a word that could give him assurance
in the midst of this vast sea of my incertitude.

–Daddy, how is it that nothing will separate us
if everything is filled with your being gone and you left
without packing my suitcase in the closet?

–Daddy, what new dream will bring me
to the side of your bed, without you there in the mornings
to hug like before?

–Daddy, when will we get back to having breakfast
like all my life, with you right there by me
passing the bread or the butter?

–How can I make my voice reach you:
Daddy, can you get the cereal down for me,
Daddy, help me with the ties of my shoes?

–Daddy, your good-bye kiss before I leave for school,
how can I still go about feeling it
on my just washed forehead?

–Daddy, and when I return from classes,
how can I still have the treat of hearing
the tap of your footsteps behind Lisa's barking
when you open the door for me?

–Daddy, when at night I close my eyes
    without having seen you,
I ask myself: what is going on that everything
    made me into halves,
like my heart split apart…?

La caja de colores del corazón de mi hijo

Pintemos algo divertido, le digo a mi hijo.
Y él, lápiz en mano, traza unas líneas curvas para las olas
Y unas líneas rectas para la casa del Lago.
Con un amarillo-limón colorea el círculo
      del sol en medio del índigo
y con unas rayas naranja sus rayos fúlgidos
sobre las aguas pardas.
Y en la esquina del papel pinta una nube
      negra para la tormenta
y pone un verde moteado en las líneas de los palos.
Ahora observo que dibuja algo así como una
      ardilla o un gato color cacao.
"Es mi perro Pirata," me dice como
      quien sobra la explicación.
"Sos todo un artista," alcanzo a decirle.
"Ahora voy a pintar la casa de mi mamá," dice.
Y frunce el ceño mientras dibuja y hace
      florecer margaritas en el jardín.
"Mirá," me señala, "esta es la casa.
Aquí está la terraza con vista al madroño
      de las flores amarillas.
Desde esa ventana de marco de madera se ve tu cuarto.
Allí están la cocina y la mesa poniéndose y tu silla.
¿Ves papá? Aquí estás leyendo.
Ahora doblo el papel y lo meto en mi bolsillo.
Es la llave para dejarte dentro."

The Box of Crayons from the Heart of my Son

Let's draw something fun, I say to my son.
And he, crayon in hand, traces curved lines for the waves
and some straight lines for the house at the Lake.
With lemon-yellow, he colors the circle of
      a sun surrounded by indigo
with orange streaks as its resplendent rays
over a dark grey lake.
And in one corner of the paper he colors
      a black cloud for the storm
and puts speckled green on the lines of stick-trees.
I notice that he is drawing something like
      a squirrel or cat in brown.
"My dog Pirate," he tells me as if no explanation is needed.
"You are such an artist," I am about to tell him.
"Now I'm going to draw Mommy's house," he says.
And scrunching up his brow while he sketches,
      makes daisies flower in the garden.
"Look," he shows me, "This is the house.
Here is the terrace and a view of the Madrono
      Tree with the yellow flowers.
From this window with the wood frame
      it's possible to see your room.
There is the kitchen and the table all set up with your chair.
See Daddy? Here you are reading.
Now I'm folding up this paper and putting it in my pocket.
It's the key to let you inside."

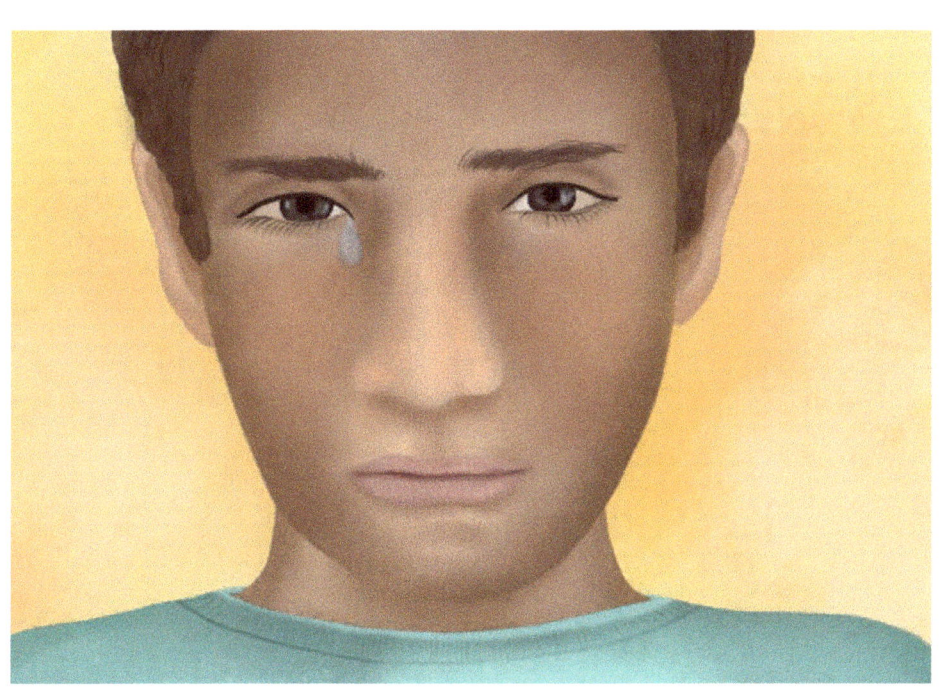

De cómo aconteció un brillo en la oscuridad

Ya sé hijo, que te estás reventando de dolor
Ya sé que estás pensando en qué fallaste.
Vos no has fallado en nada. Vos no.
Ya sé que te decía: "No llore que está bien criado"
Pero ahora no, ahora no. Soltá el llanto.
Que no te oprima lo que no está en vos resolver.
La vida a veces nos deja sin capacidad de maniobra.
Y entonces es humano preguntarse para qué esta vida,
este huracán de la ceniza, esta espesura de la noche
— la hora, la más oscura, es para amanecer—
¿Ves? así, ya está… hay luz en tus lágrimas.

On How Bright Light Occurred in the Darkness

I do know son, you are about to explode with sorrow.
I know you are thinking that you failed.
You have not failed in anything. Not you.
I know I used to say to you: "Big boys don't cry"
But now, no, not now. Let yourself sob.
Don't oppress yourself with what you cannot resolve.
At times, life leaves us with no way out.
And then it's human to ask, what point is this life,
this hurricane of ash, this dense heaviness of night
—the hour, the most dark, is just before dawn—
See? Now, there it is… there is light in your tears.

On Death and Consolation

El frasco de caramelos

Se puso a buscar un frasco de caramelos, escudriñaba el ropero entre las prótesis del pecho, las pelucas, los turbantes, los sombreros y las gorras, "mamá, ¿dónde está el bendito frasco?", y le hablaba con voz fogosa mientras abría los cajones del gavetero ocupados de medicinas y pomos de olor, hurgaba el armario del tocador donde guardaba el delineador de sus cejas que habían botado el pelo y otros varios avíos de su neceser, "mamá, no me digás que en esta vida todo es perder, ¡en algún lado lo dejaste!", la reclamaba con el ardor flameante de la fogata, pero veía su vacío en la cama, en la almohada, en el asiento frente al espejo biselado de la cómoda, la silla de ruedas en el rincón, "mamá, el vaso de vidrio con caramelos, ya sabés", y ya le salía la voz como el crac sordo de la entraña de la madera calcinada, ese leve chasquido moribundo del tizón, como volutas de humo las palabras hondas del corazón crepitando de los tucos del leño quemado, "¡mamá!, ¿qué te hiciste?", y la lágrima muda empieza a aparecer como un ratoncillo husmeando en la alacena, a la fisga entre los enseres de la cocina cobrando valor para salir, "¿te hablo de balde, mamá?" y ya la lágrima no se contiene y sale y la voz es pura ceniza porque uno nunca se acostumbra a que madre no esté.

The Jar of Caramels

He set out to find the jar of caramels, rummaging through the closet with the breast prosthesis, the wigs, turbans, caps, "Mom, where are those damn caramels?" speaking in a voice smoldering with frustration, while opening the drawers of the cabinet filled with medicine and perfumes, digging through the chest where she kept the liner for her eyebrows that had lost their hair and the other array of items from her sundry cosmetics, "Mom, don't tell me that all is lost in this life—you must have left them somewhere!" he asserted with a burning impatience, but he could see her absence on the bed, the pillow, on the seat in front of the beveled mirror of her dressing table, the wheelchair in the corner, "Mom, the jar of caramels, you know" in a voice that came out of him like a muted crack from deep inside still smoldering wood, the slight snap of a dying fire; like spirals of smoke, the words deep in his heart charred like burned remains, "Mom, where are you?" and the muffled tear begins to appear like a mouse sniffing in the cupboard, furtive among the kitchen utensils building up the courage to escape, "What is the point in talking to you, Mom?" and the tear cannot be contained, escapes, and the voice is pure ash, because no one ever becomes accustomed to a mother who is not there.

Retrato en el jardín

Lleva puesto un cotón rojo calado de flores que se abre paso en el zacate entre los frutos rubios de maracuyá y las ramas desgajadas por caimitos tintos. Los pájaros bordados de las mangas sacuden sus alas mientras recorta las veraneras blancas y azafrán, o riega las orquídeas celestes. Las flores del encaje saludan a los limones verdes y amarillos, y el colibrí volando en las flores fragantes de las limonarias ya no se sabe si es uno también agudo, ardiente, rápido, cosido con hilos de colores. Entre silbos, siseos, aleteos y matices el cotón es parte del jardín y al revés, y ella, ella sólo se distingue en el paisaje porque los ojos de una madre siempre están atentos a sus hijos como una clueca.

Portrait in the Garden

She wears a red kimono covered with flowers, passing through the grass between the golden fruit of the passion flower vine and the purple laden boughs of the caimito. The birds embroidered on the sleeves of her gown flutter their wings as she trims the bougainvillea, filled with white and saffron flowers, or gives the thunbergia, celestial blue, some water. The flowered lace on her gown greets the green and yellow lemons, and the hummingbird flying among the fragrant blossoms in the hedge of citrus becomes part of it, discerning, fiery, quick, sewn with colored threads. Among the whistles, hisses, fluttering, and mingling of colors, the kimono is part of the garden with the garden in it, while she, she is almost imperceptible but for the eyes of a mother, always alert to her children like a broody hen.

Notes for northern readers:

Maracuya is the fruit of the passion flower vine, which is a rampant climber and has magnificent red or purple flowers.

Caimito looks a bit like a plum. However, the inside is a creamy, rich dessert that is eaten with a spoon, like custard. It has many different names, depending on the tropical country; my favorite is Vú Sữa, literally translated as milky breast nipples.

Bougainvillea is a massive cloud of color when in bloom, with profusive flowers ranging from golden to deep rose or purple.

Thunbergia grandiflora is a rambling vine that produces shockingly beautiful large blue flowers, reminiscent of a phalaenopsis orchid.

La elección

Para Alex, hermano

Las cosas han variado más rápido de lo que hemos sido
(capaces de absolver.
Aunque quizás "rápido" es una manera
    de ignorar mi indigencia,
porque siendo los mismos
no nos reconocemos en lo que somos
o casi no somos lo que nos reconocemos
casi sin darnos cuenta
o sin querer darnos cuenta.

La vida que pasa (v.g.: una enfermedad incurable)
abre la celda al alma.
Pero renegamos de esa puerta que se abre
porque nos cuesta atender las señas del mundo invisible,
como si no hubiera más realidad que la
    que apenas entendemos.
Porque no gobernamos el porqué de las cosas
ni por qué las cosas no pasan
ni por qué las cosas nos pasan.
Y nuestros seres caen frágiles como tinajas
y se queda la voluntad aplastada como una hormiga.

Caminamos como si no hubiera allá,
atenidos a un allí desguarnecido y caedizo
acumulando lo fútil como si ello saciara la existencia.
Pero no hay más camino que el que no vemos.

FAMILY ALBUM: AN ILLUSTRATED GLIMPSE

La muerte está en otra parte.
Su enorme misterio nos inclina hacia ella
como el oro que sin aleación carece de resistencia.
Pero ella no alcanza hasta donde nosotros alcanzamos.

Nuestro talante desfallece sin alarde,
anegado en ese dolor hasta hace poco foráneo
que se prodiga como una cosa deleznable y fortuita.
Pero nuestra pequeñez tiene un valor insondable.
Concedo que es difícil no acobardarse hasta los tuétanos,
también nos espanta el terrible silencio de los vacíos infinitos.

Resentimos sentirnos ajenos frente al espejo
con el dolor del aquí solícito, que escapa a nuestras manos.
Mas somos más que nosotros mismos,
como una estrella de mar en el espejo de la bóveda del cielo.
Y es aquí probablemente adonde quería llegar.
Porque esa manera de ver lo propio con otros ojos
nos ayuda a no ver al otro con ojos extraños
y a ver Lo Otro con ojos propios.

Esto que te digo (¡hay donde reclinar el
       dolor!) es una invitación:
puedes tirarla a la papelera o puedes ponerte las pilas.
Es tu elección.

Choice

For Alex, brother

Things have changed faster than we have been able to forgive.
Although perhaps "faster" is a way to avoid my ambivalence,
because we are so much the same
we don't acknowledge how we are
or almost aren't what we acknowledge
almost without realizing
or without wanting to realize.

Passing life (an incurable illness) opens the enclosed soul.
But we sidestep this doorway that is opened
because we are distressed by signs of the invisible world,
as if it weren't more real than the one we scarcely know.
Because we don't control the course of things,
not the reason why things happen
nor the reason why things happen to us.
And our selves become as fragile as tinajas*
And our will ends up squashed like some ant.

We go along as if nothing more were out there
attending to the now that is vulnerable and frail,
accumulating the futile as if it could redeem existence.
But there is not another way than the one we don't see.
Death inhabits a different place.
Its enormous mystery draws us toward it
like gold without an alloy that lacks all resistance.
But death does not approach where we choose to be.

FAMILY ALBUM: AN ILLUSTRATED GLIMPSE

Our attitude weakens without any great show,
overcome by this pain that refuses to move on
spreading over all like something despicable, accidental.
But our smallness does have an unfathomable value.
I concede that it is difficult to avoid feeling fear to the core,
also the terrible silence of infinite emptiness frightens us.

Resenting, we feel distant from each other
     in front of the mirror
with the pain that concerns us now,
     escaping through our hands.
Yet we are more than just ourselves
like a starfish reflected from the vault of heaven.
And it is probably here where I wanted to arrive.
Because this way of seeing oneself with other eyes
helps us not see the other with eyes of a stranger
and to see The Other with our own eyes.

I tell you this (there is a place to put this
     pain!) as an invitation:
you can throw it away or you can take it on.
It's your choice.

*tinajas: clay urns that are buried in the ground to keep water fresh, gradually becoming porous and friable

Lo que dijo la mujer del samurái

En el viejo Japón existen antiquísimas creencias
sobre la maravilla intrincada en la palabra *nazoraëru,*
cuyo significado exotérico sería
"sustituir en el pensamiento un objeto por otro
con el fin de obtener un resultado mágico".
Poniendo esto en práctica con ahínco,
así dijo la mujer del samurái:

"Yo no tengo la fuerza para construir un templo,
en cambio, del talego de guijarros cojo uno
y lo coloco delante de la imagen de Buda
con el mismo fervor necesario para elevar un templo
y entonces mi oración es un templo".

"Pero mi pensamiento muerde el polvo
      de tu partida y nada…
y en mi pecho galopa el caballo para que
      vuelvas a mi lado y nada…
Mis ansias no te incitan como la guerra.
Mis lágrimas no te convocan como la sangre del enemigo".

What Was Said by the Samurai's Woman

In the old Japan existed many ancient beliefs
over the intricate wonder in the word *nazoraeru*
whose widespread significance would be
"substitute in thought one object for another,
with the end of obtaining a magical outcome."
Wholeheartedly putting this into practice
the samurai's woman said these words:

"I lack the strength to build a temple;
in exchange, from a bag of pebbles, I choose one
and put it in front of the image of the Buddha
with the same fervor necessary to erect a temple
and then my supplication is a temple."

"But my thought holds the dust of your
     departure and nothing…
in my heart a horse gallops to return
     you to me and nothing…
My desire does not arouse you like the prospect of war.
My tears fail to summon you like the blood of the enemy.

La revolución de las mariposas

Cuando en el 939,
Taira-no-Masakado se levantó contra la hegemonía de Kioto,
apareció un formidable enjambre de mariposas
como agitado por alguna misteriosa advertencia de la muerte.
El pueblo creyó que eran espíritus
de millares de hombres muertos en batalla.
Masakado había preparado en sigilo su revolución,
pero fue derrotado y decapitado y, según la leyenda,
su cabeza emprendió vuelo por su cuenta a Kioto.

Todo cambio empieza en silencio, toda metanoia
digamos la de un insecto de col, de una oruga pobre
que no logra cubrir su desnudez y hace su madriguera aparte,
un caparazón suspendido en la rama de un árbol,
echándose al coleto la casaca, hasta que rompe el capullo

y conoce la libertad del vuelo.

Revolution of the Butterflies

When in the year 939
Taira-no-Masakado rose up against the dominance of Kyoto
there appeared an enormous cloud of butterflies
as if beckoned by some mysterious warning of death.
The people believed they were spirits
of thousands of men dead in battle.
Masakado had prepared in stealth for his revolution,
but was defeated and decapitated, and according to legend,
his head took flight on its own to reach Kyoto.

All change begins in silence, all transformation (metanoia)
let's say of some tiny white eggs, of a poor larva
unable to cover its nakedness, so makes a lair apart,
a capsule hanging from the branch of a tree,
spinning its sheath, suspended until the chrysalis breaks

and then encounters the freedom of flight.

La consolación de la poesía

(Imitación de Boecio)

La poesía me recogió desnudo de la entraña de mi madre,
fue nodriza que llenó mi boca de su leche
y con arrullos me fue dando la seguridad de las palabras.

La poesía me hizo amar la palabra más que el oro,
me adiestró a dar pelea al palo del poder
y sedujo mi mortalidad con su túnica ceñida.

Compañera en mis caminos, la poesía
me avitualló con la debilidad invicta
de unas cuantas palabras exánimes.

The Consolation of Poetry

*(after Boethius)**

Poetry took hold of me naked in the womb of my mother.
Poetry was a wet nurse filling my mouth with its milk
and with its lullabies, giving me the assurance of words.

Poetry made me love the word more than gold,
guided me to challenge the misuse of power,
seduced my mortality with its tightly bound mantle.

Companion on my varied paths, poetry
sustained me through the unconquered weakness
of so many lifeless words.

*Who wrote *Consolation of Philosophy* in Latin as he awaited execution in A.D.525.

About the Authors

Pedro Xavier Solís is a Nicaraguan poet and essayist. He serves on the boards of directors of the Nicaraguan Academy of Language and of the Granada International Poetry Festival. *Poesia Reunida* (2012) is a selection of his poetry from 1980-2010, and *Atlas* (2017), his most recent collection, focuses on the eternal political themes of love and war. His work has been translated into Italian, Romanian, and Arabic, along with English in *Tides* (Mind made Books, 2015) translated by Suzanne J. Levine and *Worlds Within and Apart* (APAC, 2018) translated by Diane Neuhauser.

Diane Neuhauser has returned to Latin American poetry after a long career as a strategic management consultant for US corporations. She is now translating poetry from Spanish to English, with a special interest in Nicaragua. A doctoral program at Vanderbilt University in Hispanic poetry (many years ago) and recent stays in Central America have given her the impetus to turn to translating. She can be reached at Diane@NeuhauserLeadership.com.

Melissa Warp is a lecturer in the New Media Design department at Rochester Institute of Technology in New York. Along with teaching, she has worked for a variety of agencies as a designer and illustrator. The scope of her work has ranged from branding for health clinics and law firms, to print and web collateral for educational institutions and non-profit organizations. Among the variety of her clients, her favorites revolve around issues that she cares deeply about – the outdoors, fitness, local food, community development and outreach.

www.ingramcontent.com/pod-product-compliance
Lightning Source LLC
Chambersburg PA
CBHW041326110526
44592CB00021B/2836